I0413159

science for a changing world

Prepared in cooperation with the
New Hampshire Department of Environmental Services

Geochemical, Isotopic, and Dissolved Gas Characteristics of Groundwater in a Fractured Crystalline-Rock Aquifer, Savage Municipal Well Superfund Site, Milford, New Hampshire, 2011

By Philip T. Harte

Open-File Report 2013–1089

U.S. Department of the Interior
U.S. Geological Survey

U.S. Department of the Interior
SALLY JEWELL, Secretary

U.S. Geological Survey
Suzette M. Kimball, Acting Director

U.S. Geological Survey, Reston, Virginia: 2013

For more information on the USGS—the Federal source for science about the Earth, its natural and living resources, natural hazards, and the environment—visit *http://www.usgs.gov* or call 1–888–ASK–USGS

For an overview of USGS information products, including maps, imagery, and publications, visit *http://www.usgs.gov/pubprod*

To order this and other USGS information products, visit *http://store.usgs.gov*

Suggested citation:
Harte, P.T., 2013, Geochemical, isotopic, and dissolved gas characteristics of groundwater in a fractured crystalline-rock aquifer, Savage Municipal Well Superfund site, Milford, New Hampshire, 2011: U.S. Geological Survey Open-File Report 2013–1089, 25 p., http://pubs.usgs.gov/of/2013/1089/.

Acknowledgments

This study was conducted as part of the remedial effort at the Savage Municipal Well Superfund site, specifically operable unit 3 (OU3), and is a collaborative effort between Federal, State, and local governments, and private companies and individuals. The author wishes to thank Robin Mongeon, project manager for the New Hampshire Department of Environmental Services (NHDES); and Richard Hull, site remedial project manager for the U.S. Environmental Protection Agency (USEPA), region 1, for their leadership in managing remedial efforts and their support. Thanks to Sharon Perkins also of the NHDES for assistance in planning and sampling of residential wells. Thanks also to personnel at Roy F. Weston, Inc., for much-needed logistical assistance and sampling of monitoring wells.

Contents

Figures

Tables

Conversion Factors, Datums, and Abbreviations

Inch/Pound to SI

Multiply	By	To obtain
Length		
inch (in.)	2.54	centimeter (cm)
foot (ft)	0.3048	meter (m)
mile (mi)	1.609	kilometer (km)
Volume		
gallon (gal)	3.785	liter (L)
liter (L)	33.82	ounce, fluid (fl. oz)
Flow rate		
cubic foot per second (ft^3/s)	0.02832	cubic meter per second (m^3/s)
gallon per minute (gal/min)	0.06309	liter per second (L/s)
Concentration		
micrograms per liter (μg/L)	1.00	parts per billion (ppb)
milligrams per liter (mg/L)	1.00	parts per million (ppm)
Mass		
kilogram (kg)	2.205	pound avoirdupois (lb)
megagram (Mg)	1.102	ton, short (2,000 lb)

Temperature in degrees Celsius (°C) may be converted to degrees Fahrenheit (°F) as follows:
°F=(1.8×°C)+32

Temperature in degrees Fahrenheit (°F) may be converted to degrees Celsius (°C) as follows:
°C=(°F−32)/1.8

Vertical coordinate information is referenced to the National Geodetic Vertical Datum of 1929 (NGVD 29). Horizontal coordinate information is referenced to the North American Datum of 1983 (NAD 83).

Altitude, as used in this report, refers to distance above the vertical datum.

Volumes of liquid are given in milliliters (mL)

Delta notation for reporting of isotope data.—Stable isotope data are reported as a ratio relative to the ratio of a standard. For example, $^{18}O/^{16}O$ of a sample is compared with $^{18}O/^{16}O$ of a standard by the relation: $\delta^{18}O$ = (Rsample/Rstandard − 1) × 1,000, where Rsample = $^{18}O/^{16}O$ in the sample, Rstandard = $^{18}O/^{16}O$ in the standard, and $\delta^{18}O$ = relative difference in concentration, in parts per thousand (per mil).

Delta ^{18}O ($\delta^{18}O$) is referred to as delta notation and is the value reported by isotopic laboratories for stable isotope analysis. Delta D (also designated as δ^2H) or deuterium can be derived by analogy to $\delta^{18}O$ where the ratio ^2H:H replaces ^{18}O:^{16}O in Rsample and Rstandard. In this report deuterium is expressed as δD. The standard used for determining $\delta^{18}O$ and δD in water originally was standard mean ocean water (SMOW) as defined by Craig (1961). The standard used in this report is Vienna standard mean ocean water (VSMOW). If $\delta^{18}O$ and δD samples contain more of the heavier isotopes (^{18}O or ^2H) than the reference material, the samples have positive per mil values and are referred to as heavier than the reference material or as being enriched in the heavier isotope. Conversely, if the samples contain more of the lighter isotopes (^{16}O or H) than the reference material, the samples have negative per mil values and are referred to as lighter than the reference material or as being depleted in the heavier isotope. For example, a $\delta^{18}O$ value of −18.15 per mil can be referred to as lighter than VSMOW or depleted in ^{18}O relative to VSMOW. Once the reference material has been specified, it is assumed by convention that all values are reported relative to it unless otherwise indicated.

Dissolved inorganic carbon (DIC) of carbon-13 ($\delta^{13}C$) is reported relative to the Vienna Peedee Belemnite (VPDB) standard and expressed in per mil. The carbon-13 standard is −25 per mil VPDB; VPDB is the carbonate standard derived from the Rostrum of Belemnitella Americana of the Peedee Formation in South Carolina. Because values are reported relative to the reference material, samples with positive per mil values are referred to as heavier than the reference material or as being enriched in the heavier isotope. Conversely, if the samples contain more of the lighter isotopes than the reference material, the samples have negative per mil values and are referred to as lighter than the reference material or as being depleted in the heavier isotope.

Abbreviations

Ar	argon
As	arsenic
C	carbon
CH_4	methane
CHF	Campbell Hill Fault
CO_2	carbon dioxide
DO	dissolved oxygen (dissolved water sample)
GMWL	global meteoric water line
gpm	gallons per minute
H	hydrogen
LMWL	Local meteoric water line
meq/L	milliequivalents per liter
µg/L	micrograms per liter
MSGD	Milford-Souhegan Glacial Drift
N_2	nitrogen
NHDES	New Hampshire Department of Environmental Services
NWIS	National Water Information System
‰	per mil (parts per thousand)
O_2	oxygen (dissolved gas sample)
ORP	oxidation-reduction potential
OU	operational or operable unit
PCE	tetrachloroethylene
R	reference standard
R^2	coefficient of determination
RDL	reported detection level
RT	recharge temperature
Ur	uranium
USEPA	U.S. Environmental Protection Agency
USGS	U.S. Geological Survey
VDPB	Vienna Peedee Belemnite
VSMOW	Vienna standard mean ocean water
$\delta^{13}C$	delta of carbon-13
$\delta^{18}O$	delta of oxygen-18 isotope
δD	delta of deuterium (^2H)

Geochemical, Isotopic, and Dissolved Gas Characteristics of Groundwater in a Fractured Crystalline-Rock Aquifer, Savage Municipal Well Superfund Site, Milford, New Hampshire, 2011

By Philip T. Harte

1 Introduction

Tetrachloroethylene (PCE), a volatile organic compound, was detected in groundwater from deep (more than (>) 300 feet (ft) below land surface) fractures in monitoring wells tapping a crystalline-rock aquifer beneath operable unit 1[1] (OU1) of the Savage Municipal Well Superfund site (Weston, Inc., 2010). Operable units define remedial areas of contaminant concern. PCE contamination within the fractured-rock aquifer has been designated as a separate operable unit, operable unit 3 (OU3; Weston, Inc., 2010). PCE contamination was previously detected in the overlying glacial sand and gravel deposits and basal till, hereafter termed the Milford-Souhegan glacial-drift (MSGD) aquifer (Harte, 2004, 2006). Operable units 1 and 2[2] encompass areas within the MSGD aquifer, whereas the extent of the underlying OU3 has yet to be defined. The primary original source of contamination has been identified as a former manufacturing facility—the OK Tool manufacturing facility; hence OU1 sometimes has been referred to as the OK Tool Source Area (New Hampshire Department of Environmental Services, undated).

A residential neighborhood of 30 to 40 houses is located in close proximity (one-quarter of a mile) from the PCE-contaminated monitoring wells (fig. 1). Each house has its own water-supply well installed in similar rocks as those of the monitoring wells, as indicated by the New Hampshire State geologic map (Lyons and others, 1997). An investigation was initiated in 2010 by the U.S. Environmental Protection Agency (USEPA) region 1, and the New Hampshire Department of Environmental Services (NHDES) to assess the potential for PCE transport from known contaminant locations (monitoring wells) to the residential wells.

The U.S. Geological Survey (USGS) and the NHDES entered into a cooperative agreement in 2011 to assist in the evaluation of PCE transport in the fractured-rock aquifer. Periodic sampling over the last decade by the USEPA and NHDES has yet to detect PCE in groundwater from the residential-supply wells (as of 2012). However, part of assessing the potential for PCE transport involves understanding the origin of the groundwater in the monitoring and residential wells. One of the tools in delineating the movement of groundwater to wells, particularly in complex, highly heterogeneous fractured-rock aquifers, is the understanding of the geochemical and isotopic composition of groundwater (Lipfert and Reeve, 2004; Harte and others, 2012). This report summarizes findings from

---

[1]OU1 designates the primary source area of PCE for the Savage Municipal Well Superfund site.
[2]OU2 designates the extended plume area of PCE for the Savage Municipal Well Superfund site.

analyses of geochemical, isotopic, and dissolved gas characteristics of groundwater. Samples of groundwater were collected in 2011 from monitoring wells and nearby residential-supply wells in proximity to OU1.

1.1 Well Construction

Construction information on the sampled wells (table 1) was derived from driller logs for the monitoring wells and from NHDES reports for the residential wells (Genevieve Al-Egaily, New Hampshire Department of Environmental Services, written commun., August 2, 2010). Most monitoring wells also were logged with a suite of borehole geophysical tools, which helped verify well construction information (Weston, Inc., 2012). All sampled wells are openly connected (open borehole) to the fractured-rock aquifer. The length of each open borehole can be determined by subtracting casing length from well depth (table 1). The maximum open-borehole length, 520 ft, is at DW–24. Wells are typically cased with 6-inch-diameter steel pipe that penetrates through the overlying MSGD aquifer and extends at least 10 ft into the underlying rock.

The reported well yields ranged from 1.5 (well DW–12) to 100 (well DW–17) gallons per minute (gpm), based on drilling records (table 1). These yields may not reflect the yield capability of the aquifer under steady state conditions (equilibrium conditions) because part of the yield is likely from storage (well and aquifer) and represents a short-term (hours to days) yield. Nevertheless, reported yields are useful to assess the relative water yielding capability of each well.

1.2 Geology, Fracture Characteristics, and Lineaments

The fractured-rock aquifer consists of tonalite, granite, and gneiss (Lyons and others, 1997). Tonalite is mapped to the west and is coincident with the higher terrain in the study area. Tonalite is separated from the rocks to the east (granite and gneiss) by the Campbell Hill Fault[3] (CHF; fig. 1). The fault is primarily a normal fault that also may have a strike slip component (William C. Burton, U.S. Geological Survey, written commun., 2013). Granite and gneiss occur in the valley (Lyons and others, 1997).

The residential and monitoring wells are intersected by multiple fractures over the length of the open borehole. Mixing of groundwater, therefore, occurs in the borehole from the contribution of groundwater from multiple fractures. Mixing can complicate the analysis of results from well water samples because they represent composite (integrated) samples.

Fractures are predominantly northeast striking and steeply inclined (>45 degrees) (Weston, Inc., 2012; William C. Burton, U.S. Geological Survey, written commun., 2013). The location of the study area on the western limb of the Massabesic anticlinorium is likely a major factor in the number of foliation features that dip to the northwest (William C. Burton, U.S. Geological Survey, written commun., 2013).

Lineaments are linear features seen on the surface of the Earth with remotely sensed imagery. They are potentially related to structural features and high water–yielding zones within the bedrock (Mabee and Hardcastle, 1997). Lineaments were mapped in the study area by Clark and others (1997) and are shown on figure 1. Several wells are close (within 100 ft) to lineaments or the CHF including DW–2, DW–17, DW–12, DW–5A, DW–6, DW–9A, DW–19, and DW–18. Several of these wells (called lineament wells), DW–2 (15 gpm) and DW–17 (100 gpm), have high yields (table 1), whereas several of the other wells have relatively low yields (less than (<) 10 gpm). In contrast, four of the eight wells that are not within 100 ft of the mapped lineaments have high yields. The mean yield between

---

[3]The location of the CHF is approximate and has been remapped (William C. Burton, U.S. Geological Survey, written commun., 2013).

wells located proximal (<100 ft) and distal (> 100 ft) to lineaments or the CHF is 19.8 and 18.8 gpm, respectively. The difference is not significant at the 95-percent confidence interval (p-value of 0.477 based on t-test for unequal variance).

Table 1. Well construction for sampled wells, OU3 Savage Municipal Well Superfund site, Milford, New Hampshire.

[Well type: R, residential well; M, monitoring well. Sample type: C, general chemistry sample collected; I, isotope sample collected. Altitude of land surface is in feet (ft) above the National Geodetic Vertical Datum of 1929 (NGVD 29). gpm, gallons per minute; NHDES, New Hampshire Department of Environmental Services; OU3, operations unit 3; --, no data]

NHDES well identifier[1]	Well type	Sample type	Altitude of land surface (ft)	Length of casing (ft)	Depth of well (ft)	Well yield (gpm)
OKT_DW–17	R	C,I	303	60	240	100
OKT_DW–9A	R	C,I	290	120	360	5
OKT_DW–5A	R	C,I	285	76	340	5
OKT_DW–6	R	C,I	290	--	450	--
OKT_DW–2	R	C,I	290	130	420	15
OKT_DW–27	R	C	272	--	--	--
OKT_DW–18	R	C	295	123	320	8.5
OKT_DW–20	R	C	292	135	240	8
OKT_DW–24	R	C,I	380	180	700	10
OKT_DW–25	R	C,I	319	102	500	20
OKT_DW–23	R	C	311	102	300	5
OKT_DW–21	R	C	279	115	320	5
OKT_DW–22	R	C	300	103	320	3
OKT_DW–12	R	C,I	288	123	420	1.5
OKT_DW–19	R	C	289	112	300	3.5
OKT_DW–29	R	C,I	265	95	300	75
OKT_DW–30	R	C	265	100	500	25
OKT_DW–28	R	C	275	--	--	--
OKT_BR–4	M	C,I	269	138	420	--
OKT_MW–30	M	C,I	268	160	304	--
OKT_BR–3	M	C,I	275	134	400	--

[1]The "OKT_" prefix is omitted in remainder of report. Location of wells shown in figure 1.

1.3 Well Identifier

The well identification system used in this report follows the NHDES record system (table 1 and appendix 1). The USGS uses a station (site) name identification system in addition to the NHDES identifier (appendix 1). The USGS station (site) name can be used to access well data through the National Water Information System (NWIS; http://nwis.waterdata.usgs.gov/nwis).

2 Methods of Well Sampling and Analysis

Three monitoring wells and 18 residential-supply wells were sampled in 2011 (table 1). Monitoring wells (BR–3, BR–4, and MW–30) were sampled by purging and sampling of the entire open borehole according to methods described in NHDES sample analysis plan (New Hampshire Department of Environmental Services, 2011). Typically, 50 gallons of water were purged at approximately 1 to 2 gpm prior to sampling (New Hampshire Department of Environmental Services, 2011). For a 6-inch diameter well, 50 gallons (gal) is equivalent to evacuating approximately 34 ft of water column within the open borehole. After 50 gal was purged, pump rates were decreased and sampling began. This procedure is meant to mimic a pumping cycle in a residential-supply well (New Hampshire Department of Environmental Services, 2011). All monitoring wells were previously sampled with a packer and pump assembly that allowed for the collection of samples from discrete fracture intervals (Weston, Inc., 2010); these data are discussed in the "Results of Geochemical, Isotopic, and Dissolved Gas Analyses " section below.

Residential-supply wells were sampled according to methods described in New Hampshire Department of Environmental Services (2011).Wells were purged by using the existing well pump and water system infrastructure of the home and samples collected before any household treatment system. The open boreholes of the residential-supply wells are frequently recharged from daily pumping, unlike monitoring wells, which are infrequently purged (only a few times over their well history).

Water-quality field parameters (pH, specific conductance, water temperature, oxidation-reduction potential (ORP), DO, and turbidity) were measured with an YSI Model 600XL or 6820 meter in the field. Meters were calibrated as described in New Hampshire Department of Environmental Services (2011). Water-quality field parameters were collected prior to sampling for the other chemical constituents. Only the final set of readings was recorded by field personnel (New Hampshire Department of Environmental Services, 2011). Therefore, the temporal chemical variability of groundwater during purging cannot be assessed.

Duplicate and equipment blank samples were collected according to methods described in New Hampshire Department of Environmental Services (2011). Duplicates were collected in the field immediately after initial sample collection. Laboratory spikes were performed according to NHDES laboratory procedures for most of the chemical constituents analyzed for this study.

A listing of the constituents analyzed (nonisotopic only), methods of analyses, regulatory action limits, and laboratory reporting levels is provided in table 2. In general, samples were unfiltered and collected into preacidified bottles to prevent precipitation of metals and other constituents. In addition to the chemical constituents listed in table 2, USEPA and NHDES routinely sample for volatile organic compounds (USEPA schedule 8260). A discussion of volatile organic compounds is presented in Weston, Inc. (2012). All water-quality (nonisotopic) data reported in this report also are included in the Weston, Inc. (2012) report.

Groundwaters from a subset of the residential wells (9 of the18) and all three monitoring wells were sampled, and samples were analyzed for isotopes of carbon, oxygen, and hydrogen and selected dissolved gases (fig. 1). Isotope samples were collected according to USGS procedures and analyses were performed in the U.S. Geological Survey Stable Isotope Laboratory in Reston, Va. Stable isotopes of δD were measured by using a hydrogen equilibration technique (Coplen and others, 1991; Révész and Coplen, 2008a). Stable isotopes of $\delta^{18}O$ were measured by using the CO_2 equilibration technique of Epstein and Mayeda (1953), and Révész and Coplen (2008b). Analytical results are reported as δD and $\delta^{18}O$ (per mil, relative to VSMOW) with 1-sigma uncertainties of 1 per mil for δD and 0.1 per mil for $\delta^{18}O$. These samples were collected unfiltered and untreated in 150-mL glass bottles. Dissolved inorganic carbon-13 ($\delta^{13}C$) was analyzed according to methods described in U.S. Geological Survey

4

(2012b) and St-Jean (2003). These samples were collected filtered and treated in 40-mL (milliliter) vial septum bottles.

Additional samples were collected for analysis of dissolved gases (Ar, N_2, CH_4, and CO_2). Dissolved gases were analyzed in the USGS Chlorofluorocarbon Laboratory in Reston, Va., by using gas chromatography procedures (U.S. Geological Survey, 2012a; Busenberg and others, 1998; http://water.usgs.gov/lab/cfc/). Samples were collected unfiltered and untreated in 150-mL septum bottles that were filled while submerged in water, thus without headspace.

Table 2. Chemical constituents, reporting limits and regulatory standards, OU3 Savage Municipal Well Superfund site, Milford, New Hampshire.

[All concentrations in milligrams per liter. AGQS, Ambient Groundwater Quality Standards; Env-Or-600, New Hampshire Department of Environmental Services environmental rule (September 2008); N/A, not applicable; RDL, reporting detection limit; OU3, operations unit 3; USEPA, U.S. Environmental Protection Agency;--, no standard]

Test methods	Analytes	Interim cleanup levels for Savage site	NHDES AGQS (Env-Or-600)	Lab RDLs
Total metals by USEPA method 200.7/200.8	Arsenic	0.05	0.01	0.001
	Antimony	0.003	0.006	0.003
	Beryllium	0.001	0.004	0.001
	Chromium	0.1	0.1	0.005
	Lead	0.015	0.015	0.001
	Nickel	0.1	0.1	0.005
Total metals by USEPA method 200.7/200.8	Calcium	N/A	--	1
	Iron	N/A	--	0.05
	Magnesium	N/A	--	0.1
	Manganese	N/A	0.84	0.01
	Potassium	N/A	35	0.25
	Sodium	N/A	--	1
	Uranium	N/A	--	1
USEPA method 200.7	Dissolved iron	N/A	--	0.05
USEPA 415.3	Total organic carbon	N/A	--	0.5
USEPA SM 2320B	Alkalinity	N/A	--	1
Ion chromatography, Lachat 10–117–07–1–B[1]	Chloride	N/A	--	3
Ion chromatography, Lachat 10–107–04–1–C[1]	Nitrate	N/A	10	0.05
Ion chromatography, Lachat 10–107–04–1–C[1]	Nitrite	N/A	1	0.05
Ion chromatography, Lachat 10–107–04–1–C[1]	Nitrate and nitrite	N/A	--	0.05
Ion chromatography, Lachat 10–510–00–1–E[1]	Sulfate	N/A	500	1
Ion chromatography, Lachat 10–510–00–1–E[1]	Bromide	N/A	--	0.1
Ion chromatography, Lachat 10–109–12–2–A[1]	Fluoride	N/A	4	0.2

[1]Lachat instrument (http://www.lachatinstruments.com/download/LL022-Methods-List_5-10.pdf).

3 Results of Geochemical, Isotopic, and Dissolved Gas Analyses

Results are first presented for a comparison between open-borehole samples (collected for this study) and discrete fractures samples (collected by a previous study, Weston, Inc., 2010) from the three monitoring wells. This comparison was done to assess whether open-borehole samples are representative of groundwater from the fractured rock. Water-quality field parameters (specific conductance, pH, ORP (oxidation-reduction potential), dissolved oxygen (DO), temperature, and turbidity) are discussed first, followed by a discussion of general geochemistry (major ions), isotopes, and dissolved gases. Some trace-ion chemistry was also collected (Ur, As). Uranium was detected above the reported detection level (RDL of 1 µg/L) in all samples and had a maximum concentration of 60 µg/L (Weston, Inc., 2012). Arsenic was non-detect (RDL of 1 µg/L) in all samples except for two and had a maximum concentration of 8.1 µg/L (Weston, Inc., 2012).

3.1 Comparison of Open-Borehole and Discrete Fracture Samples

The specific conductance values of well water derived from the three open-borehole samples were within the range of specific conductance from discrete fracture samples at 2 of the 3 monitoring wells (table 3). However, pH, ORP, DO, and to a lesser extent, temperature, differ between open borehole and discrete fracture samples. The pH of the open-borehole samples was less than the ranges of pH from the discrete fracture samples; the same relation was true for DO. The ORP of the open-borehole sample was within the range of ORP from fracture samples for BR–3 but outside the range for BR–4 and MW–30. Temperature from the open-borehole samples was similar in 1 of 3 wells. Uranium concentrations also were similar for both sets of samples from BR–3.

Table 3. Results of open-borehole and fracture specific samples for water-quality parameters from monitoring wells, Savage Municipal Well Superfund site, Milford, New Hampshire.
[µs/cm, microsiemens per centimeter at 25 degrees Celsius (°C); ORP, oxidation-reduction potential; mV, millivolts; DO, dissolved oxygen; mg/L, milligrams per liter; µg/L, micrograms per liter; --, no data]

Well[1]	Zone	Specific conductance range (µs/cm)	pH range	ORP range (mV)	DO range (mg/L)	Temperature range (°C)	Uranium range (µg/L)
BR–3	Discrete fracture (ranges)	206–266	8.26–8.35	-12–86	1.4–1.9	11.0–11.6	3–9
	Open borehole	237	7.18	55	0.5	12.9	7
BR–4	Discrete fracture (ranges)	222–234	8.51–8.77	67–85	1.7–3.9	9.9–11.0	--
	Open borehole	247	7.77	10	0.2	9.8	26
MW–30	Discrete fracture (ranges)	231–259	8.72–9.41	-206–32	1.9–4.1	7.9–12.5	--
	Open borehole	213	8.45	78	0.6	11.4	15

[1]Location of wells shown in figure 1.

The results of the comparison between open-borehole and discrete fracture samples suggest that the open-borehole samples may not reflect recent recharge from fractures. The purging method for the open-borehole samples is less than ideal because only 10 percent of a typical well volume is withdrawn prior to sample collection (New Hampshire Department of Environmental Services, 2011), and the samples may represent borehole water that is stagnant within the well or derived from poorly connected fractures.

The DO concentration of the open-borehole samples are approximately ⅛ to ⅓ the value of the fracture samples. The open-borehole samples likely contain some stagnant borehole water or water derived from poorly connected fractures. The median DO concentration in water from 115 residential-supply wells in New England crystalline rocks was 1.9 mg/L (Flanagan and others, 2012); the DO concentration in water from fracture samples (table 3) were comparable to residential-supply well samples from this study. The amount of stagnant water in residential-supply wells should be relatively low and, therefore, the similarity in DO concentrations in residential and fracture samples supports the theory of recent recharge from fractures (hydraulically connected fractures) in both sets of samples. In New England crystalline-rock aquifers, an inverse relation has been demonstrated between residence time and DO concentrations in groundwater: old waters had low DO concentrations. This also supports the theory of low DO concentrations in poorly connected fractures (Harte and others, 2008).

3.2 Water-Quality Field Parameters

Specific conductance, pH, ORP, DO, turbidity, and water temperature are physiochemical properties of water that can affect the mobility of trace elements in groundwater (Flanagan and others, 2012). These properties vary in water from the crystalline-rock aquifer at the site depending on the physical and chemical characteristics of soil and of aquifer materials, fracture flow (such as whether water being pumped originates from short or long flowpaths), residence time of groundwater, and inputs from anthropogenic sources such as road salting and septic leachate. Water-quality field parameters may also be affected by the frequency and amount of water withdrawn from the well and how the sample was collected.

Given the differences in the number of samples between monitoring and residential-supply wells, it is to be expected that the ranges in values of field parameters were much larger for the residential-supply well samples than the monitoring well samples, particularly for DO and turbidity (table 4). The DO of the samples from monitoring wells was less than 1 mg/L, whereas 6 of 18 samples from the residential-supply wells were greater than 1 mg/L. Differences in withdrawals between monitoring and residential wells likely affect DO, as discussed in section 3.1 (Water-Quality Field Parameters). Turbidity was much greater in the monitoring well samples than in the residential-supply well samples. A high of 801 NTU (nephelometric turbidity units) was measured at MW–30 (fig. 1).

Table 4. Results of open-borehole samples for water-quality parameters from monitoring wells and residential-supply wells, Savage Municipal Well Superfund site, Milford, New Hampshire.
[DO, dissolved oxygen; mg/L, milligrams per liter; mV, millivolts; µs/cm, microsiemens per centimeter at 25 degrees Celsius (°C); NTU, nephelometric turbidity units; ORP, oxidation-reduction potential; <, less than]

Well	Number of wells	Specific conductance range (µs/cm)	pH range	ORP range (mV)	DO range (mg/L)	Temperature range (°C)	Turbidity range (NTU units)
Monitoring	3	213–247	7.18–8.45	10–55	0.2–0.6	9.8–12.9	28–801
Residential	18	142–328	6.94–8.22	-7–185	*0.2–8.3	10.8–15.3	<1–13

*DO concentrations in 6 of 18 samples were greater than 1 mg/L.

3.3 Major-Ion Geochemical Analysis

Major-ion chemistry is useful for the designation of water type and identification of general water composition and reactions. Piper (trilinear) diagrams (Piper, 1944) are a helpful visual tool in the identification of water type; they include two ternary diagrams, one for major cations and the other for major anions in percentage of major ions in milliequivalents per liter (meq/L). The position of the water composition of the sampled water on the two ternary diagrams is then projected onto a third diagram.

Water type was identified for the sampled groundwater and compared to four parameters associated with each well: altitude of land surface (elevation), well depth, yield, and rock type. Rock type was differentiated based on the location of wells relative to three geologic features: either granite or gneiss rocks, proximity to fracture zone (within 100 ft), and tonalite rock as mapped according to the geologic map of New Hampshire (Lyons and others, 1997).

Results show groundwater ranges from a calcium-bicarbonate water type to a sodium-bicarbonate water type (fig. 2). The composition and distribution of water types suggests groundwater is chemically evolving as a result of cation exchange of calcium with sodium. Therefore, groundwater characterized as a calcium-bicarbonate water type can be viewed as relatively "chemically immature" whereas groundwater characterized as a sodium-bicarbonate water type can be viewed as relatively "chemically mature." For the fractured-rock aquifer at this site, chemically mature water essentially means that some of the groundwater from a single or multiple fractures had sufficient time for cation exchange reactions to occur.

The water type at monitoring wells BR–4 and MW–30 indicate a relatively chemically mature water composition. In addition, the relatively high pH of these waters (table 3) is consistent with more highly evolved water from the crystalline-rock aquifers of New England (Flanagan and others, 2012). Wells BR–4 and MW–30 are between the residential wells and monitoring well BR–3 (fig. 1). BR–3 had high PCE concentrations (>10,000 µg/L), BR–4 had no detectable PCE, and MW–30 had low concentrations (<100 µg/L) (Weston, Inc., 2012).

Depth of well and well yield appear to be a factor in water type, whereas the elevation of the well (altitude of land surface) and rock type show no particular water compositional pattern (fig. 3). Depth of well shows an inverse pattern with deep wells characterized as a calcium-bicarbonate water type; this suggests that the recharge water to these wells is relatively chemically immature. Although this relation appears contradictory, it is consistent with observations of water chemistry from deep wells with long open boreholes in fractured-rock aquifers (Harte and others, 2008). The deep wells generally are characteristic of low fracture frequency and low yields. In some cases, these wells have been shown to be recharged primarily by shallow fractures near the well casing, and the absence of fractures in the rock dictates that long open boreholes be drilled to ensure adequate storage for water-supply use. The pattern for yield shows that high-yield wells are primarily characterized as a calcium-bicarbonate water type, which indicates these wells were quickly recharged by relatively young groundwater (fig. 3).

3.4 Isotopic Analysis

Deuterium (δD) and oxygen-18 ($\delta^{18}O$) provide information on sources of recharge to groundwater and show a high degree of correlation. Craig (1961) demonstrated this relation by the creation of a Global Meteoric Water Line (GMWL), expressed by the equation: $\delta D = 8\ \delta^{18}O + 10\text{‰}$. The GMWL is an average of many local relations of δD and $\delta^{18}O$. Differential fractionation of δD and $\delta^{18}O$ occurs as a function of humidity during primary evaporation of water vapor from the ocean and as a function of temperature during secondary evaporation as rain falls from a cloud (Kendall and Coplen, 2000). These two factors affect the local relation of δD and $\delta^{18}O$, thereby producing a unique Local Meteoric Water Line (LMWL) at different locations (Benjamin and others, 2004). Kendall and Coplen (2000) developed an LMWL for New Hampshire that is expressed as $\delta D = 7.3\ \delta^{18}O + 5.3\text{‰}$. The latter LMWL is presented in selected graphs shown in this report. The values of $\delta^{18}O$ and δD from precipitation are always negative because the reference standard (VSMOW) reflects the average isotopic composition of the ocean and distillation from evaporation leaves a residue of water with a heavy isotopic composition.

Measured δD and $\delta^{18}O$ values from samples plot closely to the LMWL indicating that groundwater is recharged by meteoric water. Measured δD values varied by –4.37‰ and $\delta^{18}O$ varied by –0.68‰. The δD and $\delta^{18}O$ composition of groundwater from sampled wells are similar to values in river water for the northeastern United States (Kendall and Coplen, 2000) suggesting that groundwater from the study area was recently (less than 40 years) recharged. The isotopically lightest groundwater was from well DW–6 and the isotopically heaviest from well DW–5A. Wells DW–6 and DW–5A are closely located (fig. 1) but their water quality differs the most. Results illustrate the effect of heterogeneity in fractured-rock aquifers on groundwater flow and transport.

There is no distinguishing difference between the δD and $\delta^{18}O$ composition of groundwater from the monitoring wells and many of the residential wells (fig. 4A). Groundwater from the monitoring wells had intermediate δD and $\delta^{18}O$ values. Parameters associated with each well such as rock type, elevation of well (land surface), casing length, and depth of well showed no discernible pattern. However, wells with the highest yields tended to have isotopically lighter δD and $\delta^{18}O$ values (fig. 4B).

The relation of yield to isotopic composition suggests that there is a temporal difference in recharge to some of the wells. Evapotranspiration in the warmer months preferentially distills δD and $\delta^{18}O$ and produces a heavier isotope. Conversely, winter or early spring recharge from snowmelt produces a lighter isotope. Long-term averaging of recharge would produce intermediate δD and $\delta^{18}O$ values. Samples from the monitoring wells exhibit an intermediate δD and $\delta^{18}O$ composition, indicating a diffuse recharge pattern. The highest yielding wells likely receive a part of their recharge from a shorter "seasonal" time period unlike lower yielding wells, which likely receive diffuse recharge over a longer time period (years). In this study, the highest yielding wells likely receive a greater component of recharge from the preceding winter or early spring period (sampling occurred in August 2011). The exception is DW–17, which has an intermediate δD and $\delta^{18}O$ composition that points to a bimodal (with equal contributions of light and heavy isotopes) mixing pattern of recharge. Groundwater with the heaviest δD and $\delta^{18}O$ values (DW–5A, DW–12, and DW–9A) may receive a disproportionate part of their recharge from the summer compared to other wells with lighter isotopic composition.

Dissolved inorganic carbon (DIC) $\delta^{13}C$ can help identify carbon sources and carbon reactions such as calcite dissolution. Carbon has two stable, naturally occurring isotopes: $\delta^{12}C$ (98.89 percent) and $\delta^{13}C$ (1.11 percent). The $\delta^{13}C$ of the atmosphere is $-7‰$. During photosynthesis, the carbon that becomes fixed in plant tissue is significantly depleted in $\delta^{13}C$ relative to the atmosphere (Kendall and others, 1995). Isotope fractionation in the CO_2–HCO_3–$CaCO_3$ geochemical system results in calcite that is enriched in $\delta^{13}C$ by about $10‰$ relative to CO_2 at 20°C. The $\delta^{13}C$ values of dissolved inorganic carbon (DIC) in groundwater are generally in the range of -5 to $-25‰$ (Mills, 1988; Kendall and others, 1995). The primary reactions that produce DIC are (1) weathering of carbonate minerals by acidic rain or other strong acids, (2) weathering of silicate minerals by carbonic acid produced by the dissolution of biogenic soil CO_2 by infiltrating rain water; and, (3) weathering of carbonate minerals by carbonic acid.

Under favorable conditions, carbon isotopes can be used to understand the biogeochemical reactions controlling alkalinity in watersheds (Mills, 1988; Kendall and others, 1995). Carbon isotopes can also be useful tracers of the seasonal and discharge-related contributions of different hydrologic flowpaths to streamflow (Kendall and others, 1995). In many carbonate-poor watersheds, waters along shallow flowpaths in the soil zone have characteristically light $\delta^{13}C$ values reflecting carbonic-acid weathering of silicates. Waters along deeper flowpaths within less weathered materials have intermediate $\delta^{13}C$ values characteristic of carbonic-acid weathering of carbonates (Bullen and Kendall, 1998). Other processes that may complicate the interpretation of the $\delta^{13}C$ values of surface waters and groundwater include CO_2 degassing, input of soil gas CO_2 from bacteria respiration, carbonate precipitation, exchange with atmospheric CO_2, carbon uptake by aquatic organisms, methanogenesis, and methane oxidation (Bullen and Kendall, 1998).

Groundwater $\delta^{13}C$ varied by approximately $-20‰$, which is a fairly large range that indicates differences in contact time between the sampled groundwater and the various sources (carbonate minerals) or sinks of carbon (fig. 5). The contact time of groundwater is thought to be a limiting factor in $\delta^{13}C$ composition rather than reaction time because reaction time is fairly quick in carbonate reactions (Kendall and others, 1995). In this report, contact time is defined as the interaction of spatiotemporal factors (flowpath length and travel time) with rock mineralogy. Therefore, differences in $\delta^{13}C$ values reflect differences in flowpaths to the wells. Differences also are attributable to the effect of soil CO_2 on groundwater, which generally lowers values of $\delta^{13}C$ in groundwater to an equivalent $\delta^{13}C$ value of the predominant organic matter in the soil (Doctor and others, 2008).

Monitoring well MW–30 ($-5.09‰$) is relatively enriched in $\delta^{13}C$, which means groundwater from the well likely reacted with carbonate minerals. Conversely, DW–5A is relatively light in $\delta^{13}C$ indicating little or less reaction with carbonates and/or substantial input of groundwater affected by soil gas CO_2. Interestingly, DW–5A was isotopically heaviest in δD and $\delta^{18}O$ indicating the well was recharged by shallow groundwater that was exposed to evapotranspiration during the summer months. Monitoring wells BR–3 and BR–4 have isotopically similar $\delta^{13}C$ composition as many of the residential wells.

3.5 Dissolved Gas Analysis

Dissolved gas measurements also are useful for the determination of geochemical reactions along flowpaths. Analysis of dissolved gases, particularly noble gases, allow for the determination of recharge areas and seasonal period of recharge that the sample entered the groundwater. Other dissolved gases help identify biogeochemical reactions like methanogenesis and denitrification.

The concentrations of dissolved gases, as specified by the mean and standard deviation from repeated measurements of the same gas samples, are provided in table 5. Oxygen concentrations were generally less than 0.5 mg/L, which is consistent with water-quality field measurements of DO although biological oxygen demand could suppress DO in lab measurements. Methane generally was low (except for groundwater at MW–30) indicating low methanogenic activity. Conversely, CO_2 shows a two-order magnitude range in values. High CO_2 occurred at DW–17, which is the highest yielding well (100 gpm) in the study area. High CO_2 is likely from soil production from heterotrophic oxidation of soil organic matter and respiration from plant roots (Doctor and others, 2008). Therefore, groundwater from well DW–17 exhibits characteristics of rapid recharge. Groundwater at DW–5A has moderate CO_2 concentrations and, therefore, its relatively low $\delta^{13}C$ value (section 4.2) is attributed to less contact time with calcite minerals. Groundwater at MW–30 had low CO_2 concentrations indicating little rapid recharge.

Argon (Ar) is a noble gas and its exchange with the atmosphere ceases when water enters the saturated zone (Manning, 2009). Noble gases are chemically inert and their concentrations seldom change along flowpaths. This condition allows for the use of dissolved noble gases as a marker on the time and location of recharge water as it enters the saturated zone by the ability to use this information to calculate a recharge temperature (RT) of the water as it enters the saturated zone.

Calculated RT was made from an analysis of dissolved nitrogen and argon for an assumed amount of excess nitrogen corresponding to the pressure associated with the elevation of the land surface of the well (Heaton and Vogel, 1981). Recharge temperatures ranged from 4.1°C (DW–25) to 8.1°C (DW–5A). Warmer RT indicates rapid recharge of groundwater given the time of the sampling was August 2011. Recharge temperatures compare favorably to the inverse of the $\delta^{13}C$ for most wells except DW–25 and MW–30 (fig. 6). This suggests that soil CO_2 is an important factor in $\delta^{13}C$ value because warm RT is indicative of summer recharge. A linear regression of RT and $\delta^{13}C$ excluding DW–25 and MW–30 yields a coefficient of determination (R^2) of 0.78 (fig. 6B).

Calculated RT also compared favorably to the inverse of excess air in the samples. Excess air in the samples occurs when air is entrapped in groundwater during recharge. Excess air is commonly associated with large water-table fluctuations that occur in cold months. A linear regression of RT and excess air yields an R^2 of 0.67.

Table 5. Results of dissolved gas in groundwater from monitoring and residential wells, Savage Municipal Well Superfund site, Milford, New Hampshire.

[Residential wells start with the prefix DW. Monitoring wells include BR–3, BR–4, and MW–30. All values are in milligrams per liter. Ar, argon; CH_4, methane; CO_2, carbon dioxide; N_2, nitrogen; O_2, oxygen]

Well[1]	N_2		Ar		O_2		CO_2		CH_4	
	Mean	Standard deviation	Mean	Standard deviation	Mean	Standard deviation	Mean	Standard deviation	Mean	Standard deviation
DW–17	26.59534	0.03695	0.87786	0.00070	0.31707	0.00438	10.48209	0.04336	0.00176	0.00011
DW–24	24.28567	0.00060	0.83696	0.00252	0.31245	0.00097	2.26717	0.04404	0.00740	0.00071
DW–9A	22.76611	0.12992	0.80666	0.00493	0.29447	0.00281	1.17167	0.00118	0.00000	0.00000
DW–25	25.48657	0.00506	0.86978	0.00085	0.31288	0.00278	1.07636	0.01047	0.00000	0.00000
DW–5A	24.32725	0.14455	0.80747	0.00156	0.28880	0.00208	1.45724	0.04280	0.00074	0.00020
DW–6	28.03265	0.16318	0.91068	0.00134	0.32293	0.00963	1.39997	0.00132	0.00168	0.00137
DW–2	24.14230	0.08934	0.83316	0.00301	0.35770	0.06237	1.16506	0.12831	0.00126	0.00012
DW–12	22.83133	0.02529	0.80949	0.00222	0.29972	0.01513	2.47624	0.02459	0.00000	0.00000
DW–29	22.94571	0.15744	0.80671	0.00289	0.55386	0.17658	0.87365	0.04255	0.00000	0.00000
BR–4	23.95804	0.07792	0.82741	0.00151	0.31607	0.00566	0.49936	0.01635	0.00000	0.00000
MW–30	19.62685	0.09213	0.73480	0.00405	0.28182	0.01016	0.03532	0.02207	2.94754	0.09149
BR–3	24.18718	0.02744	0.82770	0.00044	0.30076	0.01133	1.00889	0.02519	0.00589	0.00013

[1]Location of wells shown in figure 1.

4 Implications for PCE Transport

Results of the geochemical, isotopic, and dissolved gas analyses can be used to characterize the residential wells based on their potential for capturing groundwater that has traveled along long flowpaths (>¼ mile). Long flowpaths are considered necessary to transport PCE contamination from PCE source areas to the area served by the residential wells. Conversely, short flowpaths are less likely to transport PCE contamination to the residential wells given the distances between the residential wells and PCE contamination (fig. 1). A preponderance of recharge to wells from short flowpaths augments the need for wells to capture long flowpaths that potentially could be transporting PCE.

The geochemical, isotopic, and dissolved gas analyses provide information on contact time between the groundwater and the rock. The information on contact time is then used to infer flowpath length assuming that (1) contact time is analogous to travel time, and (2) travel time generally increases with increasing flowpath length. It is acknowledged that heterogeneity affects the mineralogy and permeability distribution of the fractured-rock aquifer and that contact time may not be precisely analogous to travel time or flowpath length. However, as a "rule of thumb" it is believed that there is a general overall positive relation between increasing contact time and flowpath length.

Individually and collectively, the chemical analyses can be used as a semiquantitative guide in determining flowpath length. The chemistry data are also potentially useful in identifying the amount of mixing in the open borehole. Potentially highly mixed groundwater in the residential wells likely means a greater ability to dilute contaminants if a limited subset of fractures transports PCE.

4.1 Vulnerability Rank Model

Different categories of chemical analyses are affected by different reactions or conditions. The synthesis of results can be used to develop multiple lines of evidence to identify flowpath length. Several categories of chemical analyses were used to rank the samples based on the potential of the well to capture water that had traveled along short or long flowpaths (table 6). The criteria for ranking are specified in table 6 under the predominant process for that particular analysis. For example, light isotopic $\delta^{13}C$ values are interpreted as groundwater with little contact with carbonate minerals and/or recharged rapidly from shallow sources such as groundwater showing the effect of soil gas CO_2. Therefore for $\delta^{13}C$, wells were ranked from light to heavy. Heavier $\delta^{13}C$ values would imply that the groundwater traveled along longer flowpaths. Wells more likely to intercept long flowpaths were identified under each category as those falling in the lower half (arbitrary limit) of the ranking (ranking from short to long).

The ranking for δD and $\delta^{18}O$ is more complex and relates to the relative effect of seasonal vs. long-term recharge. Groundwater samples with either light or heavy "end member" δD and $\delta^{18}O$ values were considered affected by seasonal recharge and ranked under the short flowpath category. Groundwater samples with intermediate δD and $\delta^{18}O$ values were considered representative of diffuse, average recharge and ranked under the long flowpath category. Alternatively, bimodal mixing of end member δD and $\delta^{18}O$ values from multiple water-bearing fractures could produce similar intermediate δD and $\delta^{18}O$ values. In this case, the samples ranked in other categories would provide some insight on the amount of mixing in the well.

By simply counting the number of times a well falls into the lower half of each category, a relative assessment can be made of a well's vulnerability to capture long flowpaths. Of the nine wells that were sampled for chemistry, isotopes, and dissolved gases, wells DW–2, DW–24, DW–17, and DW–6 ranked in the lower half three times and had the highest occurrences in the lower half (relative score). Therefore these four wells likely capture some groundwater from long flowpaths. Wells DW–29,

12

DW–25, and DW–9A ranked in the lower half twice and have groundwater chemical signatures that suggest possible capture of long flowpaths.

Several wells show strong characteristics of having mixed groundwater and likely capture groundwater from a variety of shallow and deep fractures. These include DW–17 (high CO_2, moderate $\delta^{13}C$ value, moderate cation exchange (major ion), and colder RT), and DW–5A (relatively heavy δD and $\delta^{18}O$ values but major ions indicate cation exchange). At DW–5A, the heavy δD and $\delta^{18}O$ values indicate groundwater is affected by evapotranspiration during the summer; groundwater recharged primarily in summer months is interpreted as recent recharge. Conversely, DW–5A also has evidence of being affected by cation exchange, which is characterized as a more chemically mature water type.

This vulnerability assessment is based on a model to evaluate flowpath length but should be tempered by the location of the well relative to the PCE contamination source. For example, although wells DW–24 and DW–25 show evidence of capturing long flowpaths, their location indicates that they receive a part of their recharge from the hillside areas to the west. Conversely, a high level of vulnerability may be appropriate for well DW–2, which is near the PCE contamination and has evidence of capturing long flowpaths (relative score of three). The flowpath length model should also be tempered by the potential for mixing of young and old groundwater in a well indicating the ability to dilute contaminants being transported by select fractures.

Table 6. Ranking of groundwater samples from wells based on results of chemical analyses and the potential of capturing long flowpaths, Savage Municipal Well Superfund site, Milford, New Hampshire.

[Monitoring wells excluding (BR–3, BR–4, and MW–30). $\delta^{13}C$, del value of dissolved inorganic carbon of carbon-13 isotope; RT, recharge temperature; CO_2, carbon dioxide; δD, deuterium; $\delta^{18}O$, oxygen-18. Shaded cells are wells more likely to capture long flowpaths; Arrow indicates direction of increasing flowpath length].

Category	Major ion	$\delta^{13}C$	CO_2	RT	δD and $\delta^{18}O$
Predominant process used for the ranking of vulnerability	Cation exchange (chemical maturity)	Carbonate (for example, calcite) dissolution and CO_2 soil gas input	CO_2 soil gas and shallow recharge	Seasonal (summer and winter) recharge	Fractionation from seasonal recharge
Ranking order	Low (short flowpath) to high (long flowpath) Na to Ca milliequivalent per liter ratio	Light (short flowpath) to heavy (long flowpath) isotopic composition	High (short flowpath) to low (long flowpath) concentrations	Warmer or colder RT (short flowpaths) to average RT (long flowpaths, and diffuse recharge)	Heavy or light (short flowpaths) to intermediate (long flowpath) isotopic composition
Short flowpaths	DW–28*	DW–5A	DW–17	DW–5A	DW–5A
	DW–25	DW–25	DW–12	DW–29	DW–6
	DW–23*	DW–9A	DW–24	DW–9A	DW–9A
	DW–22*	DW–2	DW–5A	DW–12	DW–12
	DW–29	DW–12	DW–6	DW–2	DW–29
	DW–24				
	DW–17				
	DW–30*				
	DW–27*				
	DW–12	DW–17	DW–9A	DW–24	DW–17
	DW–20*	DW–24	DW–2	DW–17	DW–25
	DW–5A	**DW–29	DW–25	DW–6	DW–2
	DW–6	DW–6	DW–29	DW–25	DW–24
	DW–2				
	DW–21*				
	DW–19*				
	DW–18*				
Long flowpaths	DW–9A				

*Sample for major ion data only.

**Heavier $\delta^{13}C$ but low alkalinity suggests mixing.

5 Conclusions

Understanding the origin of groundwater flow to fractured-rock aquifers provides a mechanism to assess the vulnerability of residential-supply wells to capture contaminants from known contamination areas. For this study, although concentrations of tetrachloroethylene (PCE) have yet to be detected in samples from nearby residential-supply wells, concerns over future changes in hydraulic stresses (pumpage) or modifications to remedial operations at operable units provided motivation to characterize groundwater from the residential–supply wells. The interpretation of geochemical and isotopic data helped researchers assess the origin of flowpaths to each well.

Groundwater samples that were collected from monitoring and residential-supply wells represent an integrated sample from multiple flowpaths and multiple fractures. Deciphering the likely origin of groundwater from each well sample required the use of multiple lines of evidence, which were provided by the suite of chemical, isotopic, and dissolved gas analyses performed for this study.

A simple vulnerability-rank model was developed that utilized the multiple lines of evidence approach based on data collected for this study. The vulnerability-rank model assumes that groundwater that appears to be younger is recharged by short flowpaths. Short flowpaths originate closer to the well. Given the distances (>¼ mile) of some of the residential-supply wells to areas of known contamination, wells characterized as containing signatures of young groundwater are assumed to be less at risk. Groundwater samples that exhibit a high level of mixing of younger and older waters are from wells that have the capability of diluting contaminants because they capture a variety of flowpaths. Groundwater that appears to be older is assumed to be recharged by long flowpaths (> ¼ mile). Long flowpaths are capable of transporting contaminants to residential-supply wells. Four wells were characterized as containing signatures of old groundwater. Two of the four wells are closer to PCE source areas and may be the most vulnerable to potential PCE contamination; these wells could be targeted for additional study to understand their fracture and flow characteristics.

Results of this work can be used to help target wells for additional chemical analyses and geophysical investigations. For example, age dating of groundwater samples with environmental tracers would refine the evaluation of flowpath length. Geophysical logging can be performed to help map fracture patterns in open boreholes and help track sources of water. Sampling of both open boreholes (this study) and discrete fractures would help researchers identify the relative contribution of fractures to the integrated open-borehole sample. Collectively, the estimates of age from groundwater samples and geophysical fracture mapping would provide additional evidence to evaluate vulnerability of residential wells to capture PCE contaminants. The vulnerability-rank model of categorical data developed by this study is most appropriate as a screening tool for followup investigations.

6 References Cited

Benjamin, Lyn, Knobel, L.L., Hall, L.F., Cecil, L.D., and Green, J.R., 2004, Development of a local meteoric water line for southeastern Idaho, western Wyoming, and south-central Montana: U.S. Geological Survey Scientific Investigations Report 2004–5126, 17 p. (Also available at http://pubs.usgs.gov/sir/2004/5126/.)

Bullen, T.D., and Kendall, Carol, 1998, Tracing of weathering reactions and water flowpaths—A multi-isotope approach, *in* Kendall, Carol, and McDonnell, J.J. eds., Isotope tracers in catchment hydrology: Amsterdam, Elsevier, p. 611–646.

Busenberg, Eurybiades, Plummer, L.N., Bartholomay, R.C., and Wayland, J.E., 1998, Chlorofluorocarbons, sulfur hexafluoride, and dissolved permanent gases in groundwater from selected sites in and near the Idaho National Engineering and Environmental Laboratory, Idaho, 1994–97: U.S. Geological Survey Open-File Report 98–274, 72 p.

Clark, S.F., Jr., Ferguson, E.W., Picard, M.Z., and Moore, R.B., 1997, Lineament map of area 2 of the New Hampshire bedrock aquifer assessment, south-central New Hampshire: U.S. Geological Survey Open-File Report 96–490, 1 sheet, scale 1:48,000.

Craig, Harmon, 1961, Isotopic variations in meteoric waters: Science, v. 133, p. 1702–1703.

Coplen, T.B., Wildman, J.D., and Chen, J., 1991, Improvements in the gaseous hydrogen-water equilibration technique for hydrogen isotope ratio analysis: Analytical Chemistry, v. 63, p. 910–912.

Doctor, D.H., Kendall, Carol, Sebestyen, S.D., Shanley, J.B., Ohte, Nobuhito, and Boyer, E.W., 2008, Carbon isotope fractionation of dissolved inorganic carbon (DIC) due to outgassing of carbon dioxide from a headwater stream: Hydrological Processes, v. 22, p. 2410–2423.

Epstein, S., and Mayeda, T., 1953, Variation of O–18 content of water from natural sources: Geochimica et Cosmochimica Acta, v. 4, p. 213–224.

Flanagan, S.M., Ayotte, J.D., and Robinson, G.R., Jr., 2012, Quality of water from crystalline rock aquifers in New England, New Jersey, and New York, 1995–2007: U.S. Geological Survey Scientific Investigations Report 2011–5220, 104 p. (Also available at http://pubs.usgs.gov/sir/2011/5220.)

Harte, P.T., 2004, Simulation of source transport of tetrachloroethylene in ground water of the glacial-drift aquifer at the Savage municipal well superfund site, Milford, New Hampshire, 1960–2000: U.S. Geological Survey Scientific Investigations Report 2004–5176, 78 p.

Harte, P.T., 2006, Effects of a remedial system and its operation on volatile organic compound-contaminated ground water, operable unit 1, Savage municipal well superfund site, Milford, New Hampshire, 1998–2004: U.S. Geological Survey Scientific Investigations Report 2006–5083, 80 p.

Harte, P.T., Ayotte, J.D., Hoffman, Andrew, Rèvèsz, K.M., Beleval, Marcel, Lamb, Steven, and Böhlke, J.K., 2012, Heterogeneous redox conditions, arsenic mobility, and groundwater flow in a fractured-rock aquifer near a waste repository site in New Hampshire, USA: Hydrogeology Journal, v. 20, no. 6, p. 1189–1201, doi:10.1007/s10040-012-0844-4.

Harte, P.T., Robinson, G.R., Jr., Ayotte, J.D., and Flanagan, S.M., 2008, Framework for evaluating water quality of the New England crystalline rock aquifers: U.S. Geological Survey Open-File Report 2008–1282, 47 p. (Also available at http://pubs.usgs.gov/ofr/2008/1282.)

Heaton, T.H.E., and Vogel, J.C., 1981, "Excess air" in groundwater: Journal of Hydrology, v. 50, p. 201–216.

Kendall, Carol, and Coplen, T.B., 2000, Distribution of oxygen-18 and deuterium in river waters across the United States: Hydrological Processes, v. 15, p. 1363–1393.

Kendall, Carol, Sklash, M.G., and Bullen, T.D., 1995, Isotope tracers of water and solute sources in catchments, *in* Trudgill, S.T., ed., Solute modeling in catchment systems: New York, John Wiley and Sons, p. 261–303.

Lipfert, Gail, and Reeve, A.S., 2004, Characterization of three water types in a fractured schist, high arsenic, watershed in Maine: 2004 U.S. Environmental Protection Agency/National Ground Water Association Fractured Rock Conference, Portland, Maine; accessed October, 15, 2012 at http://clu-in.org/products/siteprof/2004fracrock.conf/cdr_pdfs/indexed/group1/638.pdf.

Lipfert, Gail, Reeve, A.S., Sidle, W.C., and Marvinney, R., 2006, Geochemical patterns of arsenic-enriched ground water in fractured, crystalline bedrock, Northport, Maine: Applied Geochemistry, v. 21, no. 3, p. 528–545.

Lyons, J.B., Bothner, W.A., Moench, R.H., and Thompson, J.B., Jr., 1997, Bedrock geologic map of New Hampshire: U.S. Geological Survey, scale 1:250,000.

Mabee, S.B., and Hardcastle, K.C., 1997, Analyzing outcrop-scale fracture features to supplement investigations of bedrock aquifers: Hydrogeology Journal, v. 5, no. 4, p. 21–36.

Manning, A.H., 2009, Ground-water temperature, noble gas, and carbon isotope data from the Española Basin, New Mexico: U.S. Geological Survey Scientific Investigations Report 2008–5200, 69 p.

Mills, A.L., 1988, Variations in the dC–13 of stream bicarbonate—Implications for sources of alkalinity: Washington, D.C., George Washington University master's thesis, 160 p.

New Hampshire Department of Transportation, 2005, NH GRANIT 2005 1–FT color aerial photos, southeast NH: Concord, N.H., New Hampshire Department of Transportation. (Also available at http://www.granit.unh.edu/data/downloadfreedata/alphabetical/databyalpha.html.)

New Hampshire Department of Environmental Services, 2011, Sampling and analysis plan (SOP) Savage municipal water supply superfund site OU–3, 621 Elm Street Milford, N.H.: Concord, N.H., Weston Solutions, Inc.

New Hampshire Department of Environmental Services, [undated], Savage municipal water supply well: New Hampshire Department of Environmental Services, accessed October 15, 2012, at http://des.nh.gov/organization/divisions/waste/hwrb/fss/superfund/summaries/savage.htm.

Piper, A.M., 1944, A graphical procedure in the geochemical interpretation of water analyses: Transactions, American Geophysical Union, v. 25, p. 914–923.

Révész, Kinga, and Coplen, T.B., 2008a, Determination of the delta (^{2}H/^{1}H) of water: RSIL lab code 1574, in Révész, Kinga, and Coplen, T.B., eds., Methods of the Reston Stable Isotope Laboratory: U.S. Geological Survey Techniques and Methods, book 10, chap.C1, 27 p. (Also available at http://pubs.water.usgs.gov/tm10C1/.)

Révész, Kinga, and Coplen, T.B., 2008b, Determination of the delta (^{18}O/^{16}O) of water: RSIL lab code 489, in Révész, Kinga, and Coplen, Tyler B., eds., Methods of the Reston Stable Isotope Laboratory: U.S. Geological Survey Techniques and Methods, book 10, chap. C2, 28 p. (Also available at http://pubs.water.usgs.gov/tm10C2/.)

St-Jean, G., 2003, Automated quantitative and isotopic (^{13}C) analysis of dissolved inorganic carbon and dissolved organic carbon in continuous-flow using a total organic carbon analyser: Rapid Communication in Mass Spectrometry, v. 17, no. 5, p. 419–428.

U.S. Geological Survey, 2012a, Reston Dissolved Gas Laboratory: U.S. Geological Survey, accessed January 31, 2012, at http://water.usgs.gov/lab/.

U.S. Geological Survey, 2012b, Reston Stable Isotope Laboratory: U.S. Geological Survey, accessed January 31, 2012, at http://isotopes.usgs.gov/.

Weston, Inc., 2009, Draft 2009 annual report—Savage municipal well superfund site, Milford, New Hampshire: Concord, N.H., Weston Solutions, Inc.

Weston, Inc., 2010, Draft bedrock investigation and conceptual site model report Savage municipal water supply superfund site OU–1, 621 Elm Street, Milford, New Hampshire: Concord, N.H., Weston Solutions, Inc.

Weston, Inc., 2012, Draft technical memo on bedrock investigations at the Savage municipal water supply superfund site OU–1, 621 Elm Street, Milford, New Hampshire: Concord, N.H., Weston Solutions, Inc., Weston Solutions, Inc.

Figures

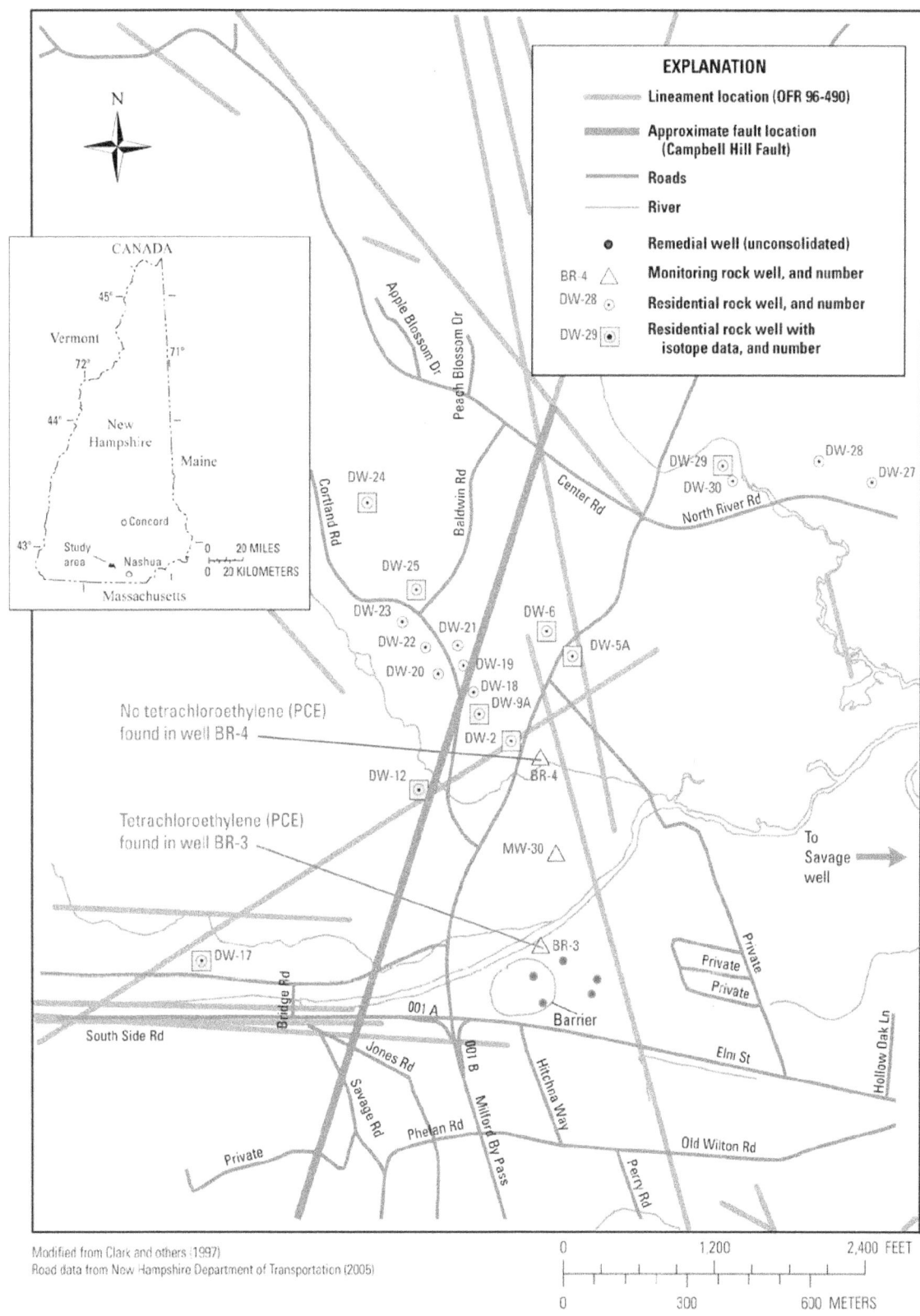

Figure 1. Location map of monitoring wells and residential-supply wells, Savage Municipal Well Superfund site, Milford, New Hampshire.

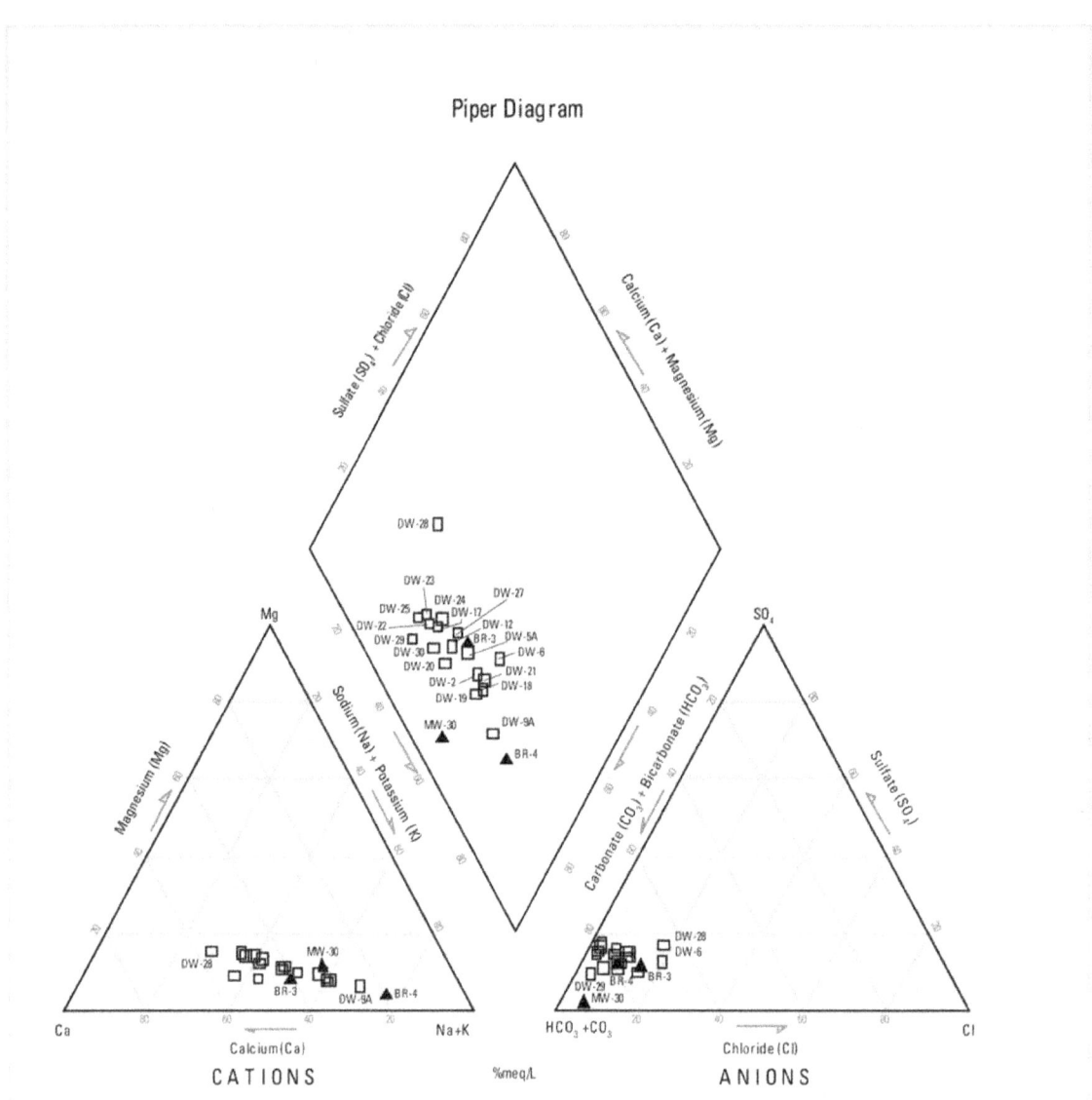

Figure 2. Piper diagram of major water type for residential and monitoring wells, Savage Municipal Well Superfund site, Milford, New Hampshire. %meq/L, percent milliequivalents per liter. Residential wells start with the prefix DW; monitoring wells include BR–3, BR–4, and MW–30.

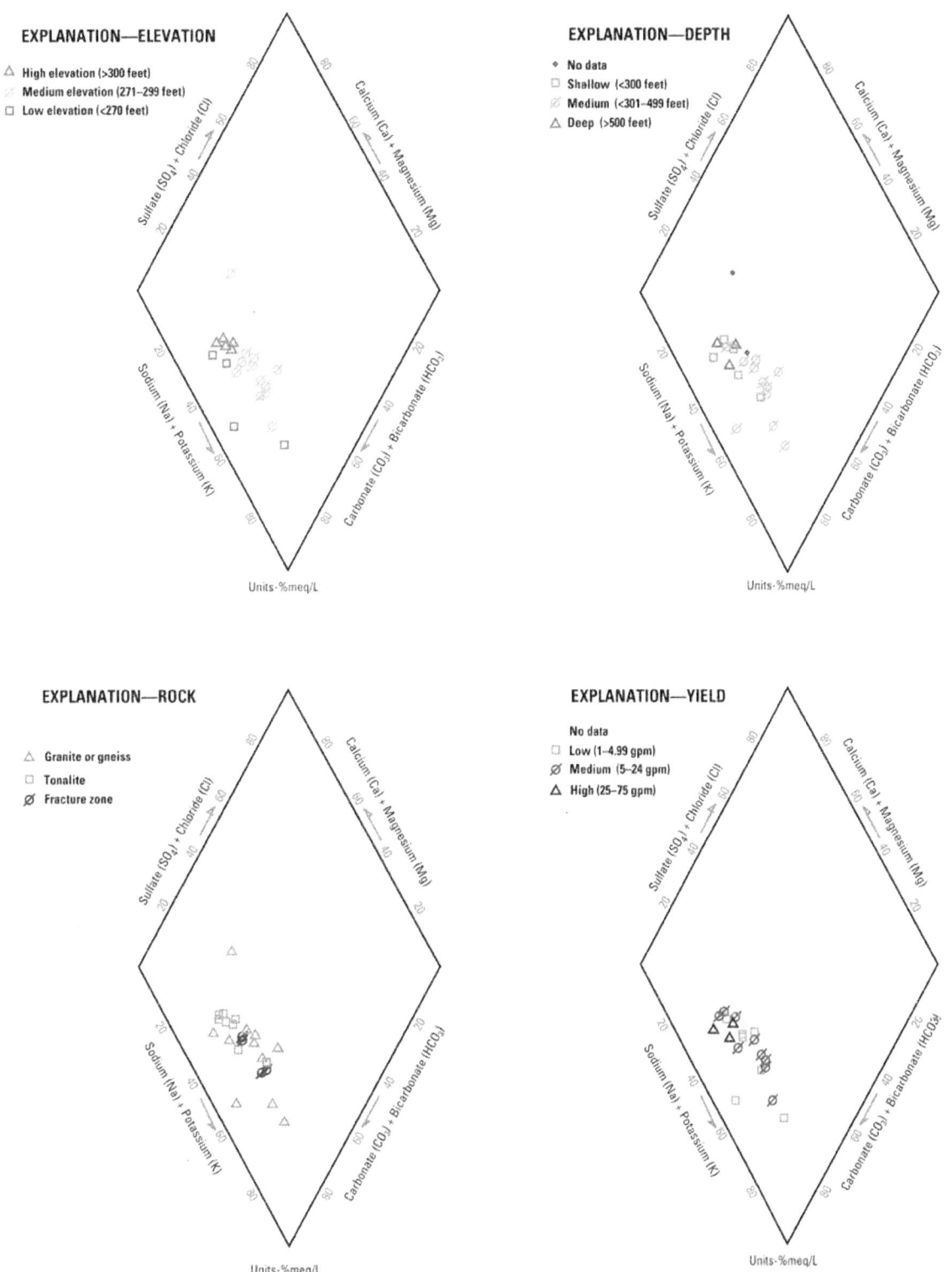

Figure 3. Modified piper of major water type (showing combined cation-anion plot only) for residential and monitoring wells, classified by well parameter, Savage Municipal Well Superfund site, Milford, New Hampshire. %meq/L, percent milliequivalents per liter; gpm, gallons per minute.

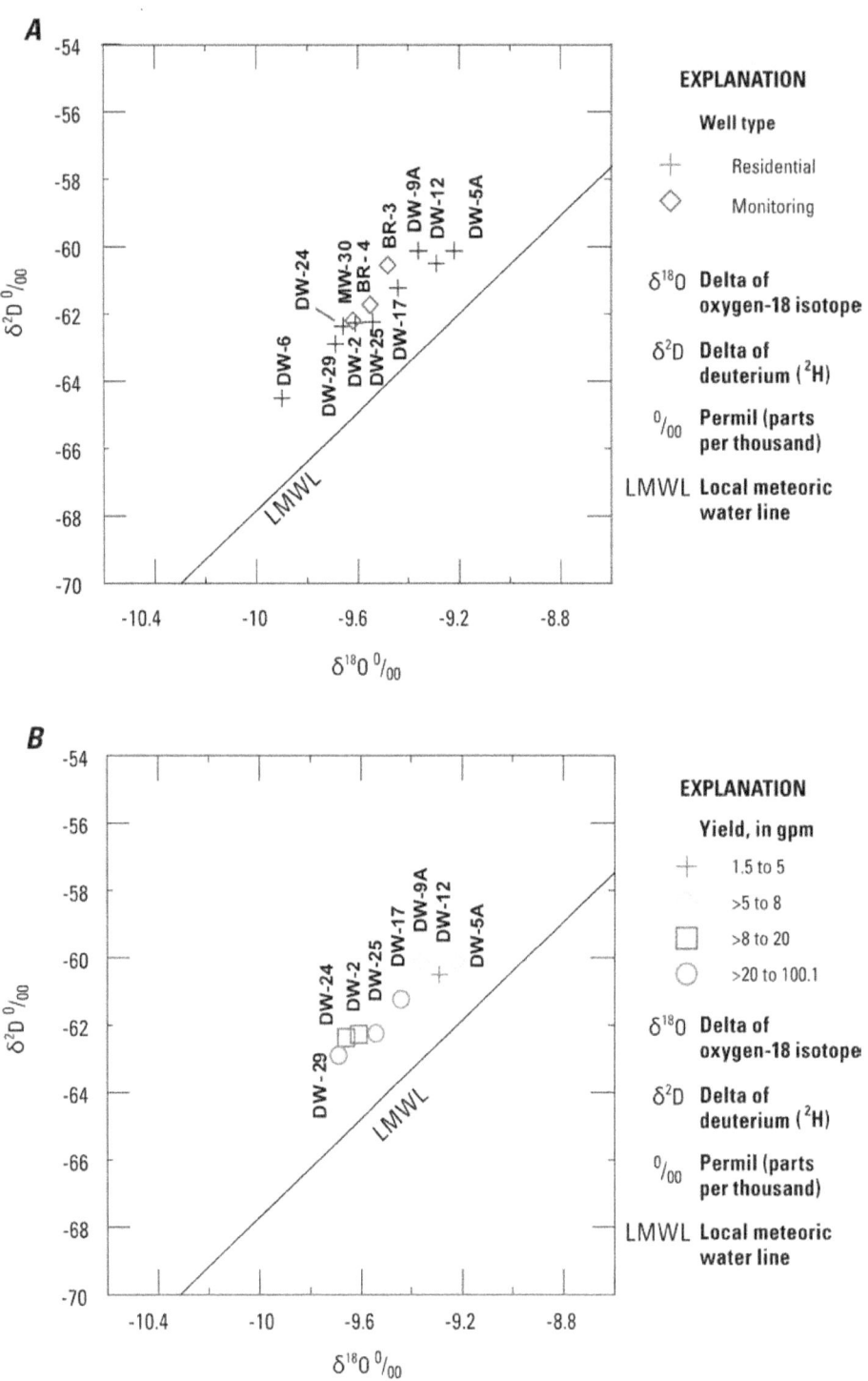

Figure 4. Graphs showing relation of stable isotopes of δD and δ18O of groundwater from residential and monitoring well samples and the local meteoric water line (LMWL) by *A,* well type and *B,* yield, Savage Superfund site, Milford, New Hampshire. gpm, gallons per minute.

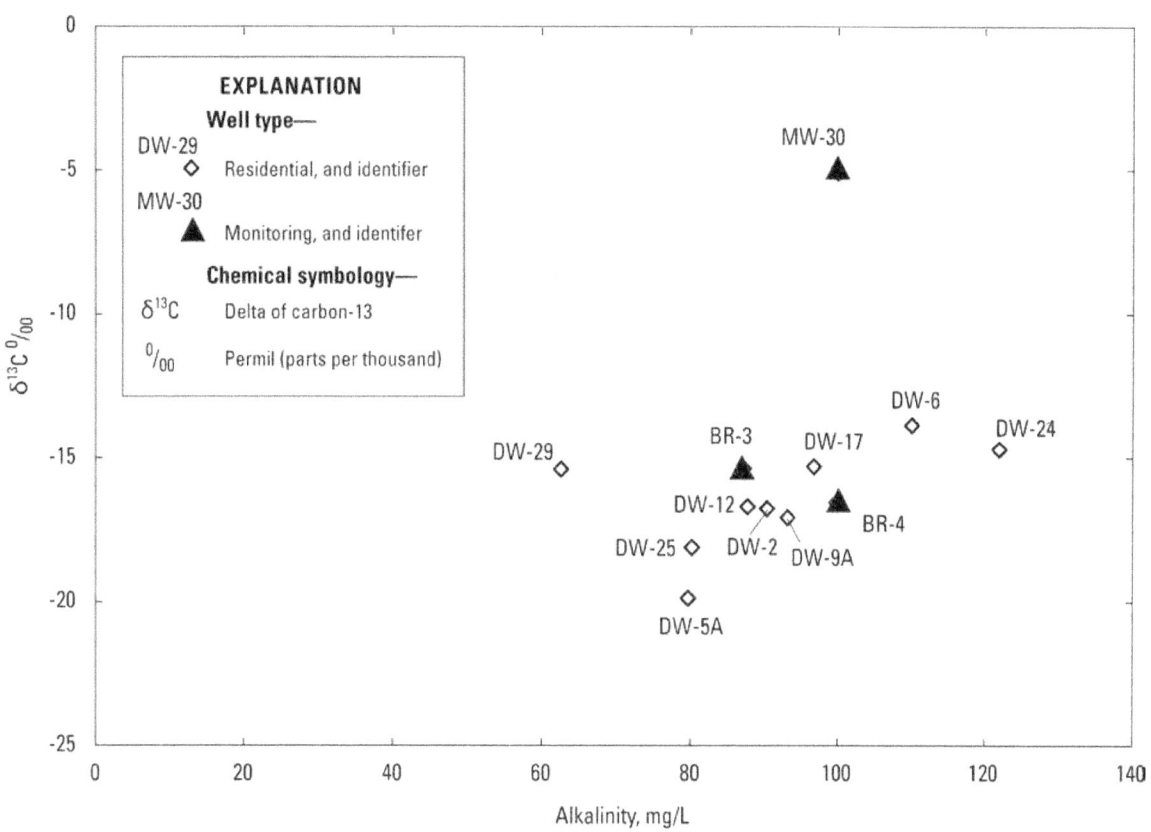

Figure 5. Graph showing relation of the delta of carbon-13 isotope ($\delta^{13}C$) and alkalinity of groundwater from residential and monitoring well samples, Savage Municipal Well Superfund site, Milford, New Hampshire.

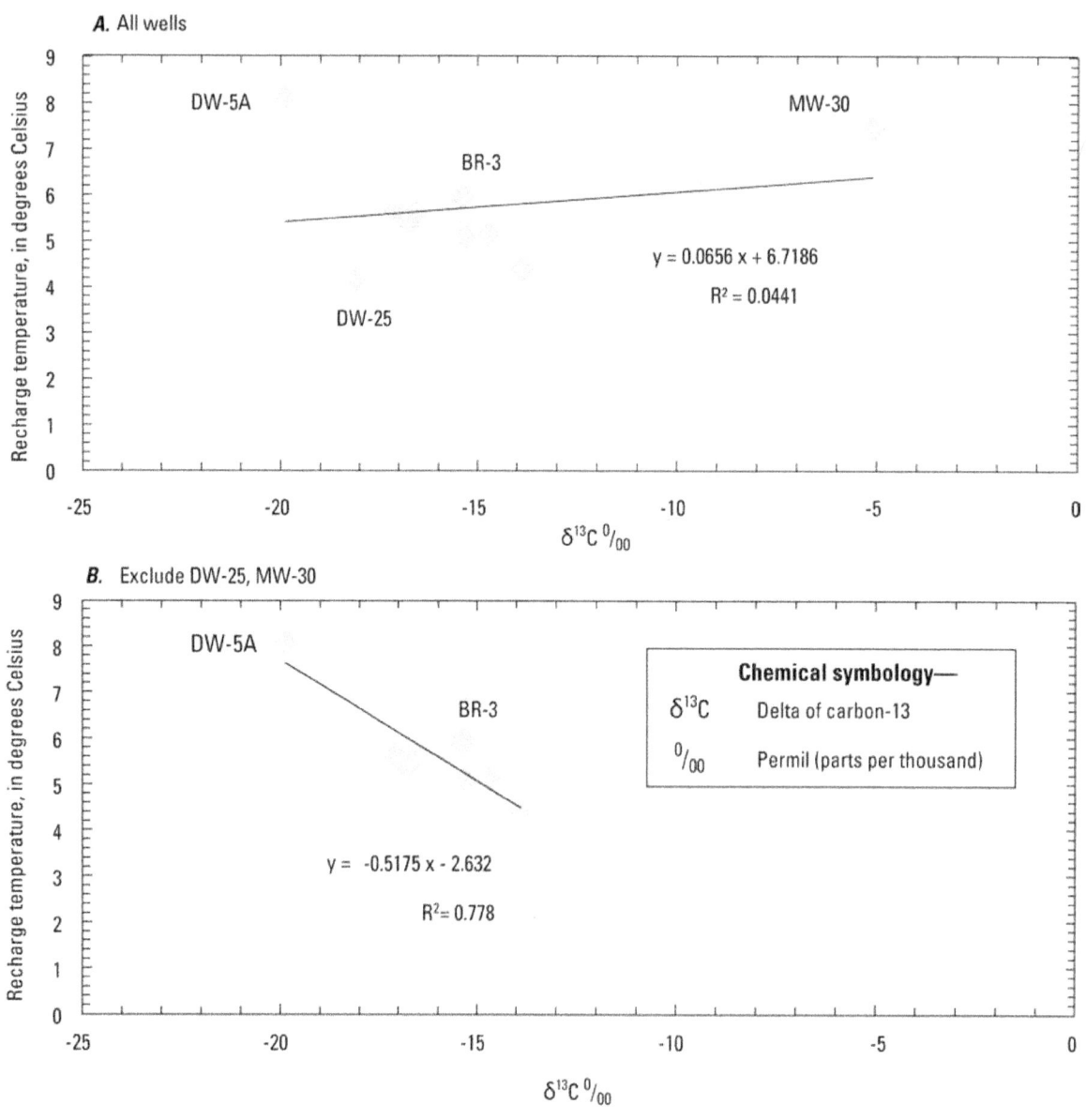

Figure 6. Graphs showing relation of recharge temperature from argon-nitrogen gas and $\delta^{13}C$ of groundwater from residential and monitoring well samples for *A*, all wells and *B*, selected wells, Savage Municipal Well Superfund site, Milford, New Hampshire. R^2, coefficient of determination.

Appendix 1.   Wells Sampled for Analysis of Isotopes

Table 1–1.   New Hampshire Department of Environmental Services and U.S. Geological Survey site identifiers for sampled wells analyzed for isotopes, OU3 Savage Municipal Well Superfund site, Milford, New Hampshire. [NHDES, New Hampshire Department of Environmental Services; USGS, U.S. Geological Survey]

NHDES well identifier	Sample collection date	USGS station (site) name
OKT_DW–25	8/30/2011	NH-MOW 445
OKT_DW–24	8/30/2011	NH-MOW 446
OKT_DW–5A	8/30/2011	NH-MOW 439
OKT_DW–2	8/30/2011	NH-MOW 440
OKT_DW–9A	8/30/2011	NH-MOW 441
OKT_DW–12	8/30/2011	NH-MOW 442
OKT_DW–6	8/30/2011	NH-MOW 447
OKT_DW–17	8/30/2011	NH-MOW 448
OKT_DW–29	8/31/2011	NH-MOW 449
OKT_BR–4	9/01/2011	NH-MOW 438
OKT_BR–3	9/01/2011	NH-MOW 437
OKT_MW–30	9/01/2011	NH-MOW 436